The Debt-Deflation Theory of Great Depressions

IRVING FISHER
1933

Professor of Economics
Yale University

The Debt-Deflation Theory of Great Depressions.

By Irving Fisher originally published in October 1933 by the Econometric Society – founded on December 29, 1930 at the Stalton Hotel in Cleveland, Ohio, whose first president was Irving Fisher.

Cornell University: "Copyright Term and the Public Domain in the United States 1 January 2009" at http://www.copyright.cornell.edu/ resources/public domain.cfm visited 2008-11-09. "Published 1923-1977 without a copyright notice. Copyright term: None. In the public domain due to failure to comply with required formalities."

ISBN 10-digit: 1453624457
EAN 13-digit: 978-1-4536-2445-6

Published 2010 by
Michael Schemmann
ThaiSunset Publications
Box 9, Pakthongchai
Thailand 30150

http://www.thaisunset.com/
Includes link to "Notification of Copyright Infringement Claim"

While quite ready to change my opinion, I have, at present, a strong conviction that these two economic maladies, the debt disease and the price-level disease (or dollar disease), are, in the great booms and depressions, more important causes than all others put together.

Irving Fisher. 1933. *The Debt-Deflation Theory of Great Depressions*. Tentative Conclusion 19 (page 22 below).

Foreword
Hat Tip to *London Banker*[1]

Thursday, 31 July 2008

Fisher's Debt-Deflation Theory of Great Depressions and a possible revision

"Panics do not destroy capital; they merely reveal the extent to which it has been destroyed by its betrayal into hopelessly unproductive works."

> - Mr John Mills, Article read before the Manchester Statistical Society, December 11, 1867, on *Credit Cycles and the Origin of Commercial Panics* as quoted in <u>Financial crises and periods of industrial and commercial depression</u>, Burton, T. E. (1931, first published 1902). New York and London: D. Appleton & Co.

I have been both a central banker and a market regulator. I now find myself questioning whether my early career, largely devoted to liberalising and deregulating banking and financial markets, was misguided. In short, I wonder whether I contributed - along with countless others in regulation, banking, academia and politics - to a great misallocation of capital, distortion of markets and the impairment of the real economy. We permitted the banks to betray capital into "hopelessly unproductive works", promoting

---

[1] Anonymous source (not copyrighted, 'unauthorized' for lack of email or address, but with great thanks): http://londonbanker.blogspot.com/2008/07/ fishers-debt-deflation-theory-of-great.html. Retrieved 2010-06-10. Posted by *London Banker* at 22:16 Labels: Debt-Deflation Theory, Irving Fisher

their efforts with monetary laxity, regulatory forbearance and government tax incentives that marginalised investment in "productive works". We permitted markets to become so fragmented by off-exchange trading and derivatives that they no longer perform the economically critical functions of capital/resource allocation and price discovery efficiently or transparently. The results have been serial bubbles - debt-financed speculative frenzy in real estate, investments and commodities.

Since August of 2007 we have been seeing a steady constriction of credit markets, starting with subprime mortgage back securities, spreading to commercial paper and then to interbank credit and then to bond markets and then to securities generally. While the problem is usually expressed as one of confidence, a more honest conclusion is that credit extended in the past has been employed unproductively and so will not be repaid according to the original terms. In other words, capital has been betrayed into unproductive works.

The credit crunch today is not destroying capital but recognising that capital was destroyed by misallocation in the years of irrational exuberance. If that is so, then we are entering a spiral of debt deflation that will play out slowly for years to come. To understand how that works, we turn to Professor Irving Fisher of Yale.

Like me, Professor Fisher lived to question his earlier convictions and pursuits, learning by dear experience the lessons of financial instability.

Professor Fisher was an early mathematical economist, specialising in monetary and financial economics. Fisher's contributions to the field of economics included the equation of exchange, the distinction between real and nominal interest rates, and an early analysis of intertemporal allocation. As his status grew, he became an icon for popularising 1920s fads for investment, healthy living and social engineering, including Prohibition and eugenics.

He is less famous for all of this today than for his one statement in September 1929 that "stock prices had reached a permanently high plateau". He subsequently lost a personal fortune of between $6 and $10 million in the crash. As J.K. Galbraith remarked, "This was a sizable sum, even for an economics professor." Fisher's investment bank failed in the bear market, losing the fortunes of investors and his public reputation.

Professor Fisher made his "permanently high plateau" remark in an environment very similar to that prevailing in the summer of 2007. Currencies had been competitively devalued in all the major nations as each sought to gain or defend export market share. The devaluation stoked asset bubbles as easy credit led to more and more speculative investments, including a boom in globalisation as investors bought bonds from abroad to gain higher yields. Then, as now, many speculators on Wall Street had unshakeable faith in the Federal Reserve's ability to keep the party going.

After the crash and financial ruin, Professor Fisher turned his considerable talents to determining the underlying mechanisms of the crash. His *Debt-Deflation Theory of Great Depressions* (1933) was powerful and resonant, although largely neglected by officialdom, Wall Street and academia alike. Fisher's theory raised too many uncomfortable questions about the roles played by the Federal Reserve, Wall Street and Washington in propagating the conditions for credit excess and the debt deflation that followed.

The whole paper is worth reading carefully, but I'll extract here some choice quotes which give a flavour of the whole. Prefacing his theory, Fisher first discusses instability around equilibrium and the influence of 'forced' cycles (like seasons) and 'free' cycles (self-generating like waves). Unlike the Chicago School, Fisher says bluntly that "exact equilibrium thus sought is seldom reached and never long maintained. New disturbances are, humanly speaking, sure to occur, so that, in actual fact, any variable is almost always above or below ideal equilibrium." He bluntly asserts:

"Theoretically there may be — in fact, at most times there must be — over- or under-production, over- or under-consumption, over- or under-spending, over- or under-saving,

6

over- or under-investment, and over or under everything else. It is as absurd to assume that, for any long period of time, the variables in the economic organization, or any part of them, will "stay put," in perfect equilibrium, as to assume that the Atlantic Ocean can ever be without a wave."

While disturbances will cause oscillations which lead to recessions, he suggests:

"[I]n the great booms and depressions, each of the above-named factors has played a subordinate role as compared with two dominant factors, namely over-indebtedness to start with and deflation following soon after; also that where any of the other factors do become conspicuous, they are often merely effects or symptoms of these two."

This is the critical argument of the paper. Viewed from this perspective we may see USA and UK decades of under-production, over-consumption, over-spending and under-investment as all tending to a greater imbalance in debt which may, if combined with oscillations induced by disturbances, take the US and UK economies beyond the point where they could right themselves into a deflationary spiral.

Fisher outlines how just 9 factors interacting with one another under conditions of debt and deflation create the mechanics of boom to bust for a Great Depression:

Assuming, accordingly, that, at some point of time, a state of over-indebtedness exists, this will tend to lead to liquidation, through the alarm either of debtors or creditors or both. Then we may deduce the following chain of consequences in nine links: (1) *Debt liquidation* leads to *distress selling* and to (2) *Contraction of deposit currency*, as bank loans are paid off, and to a slowing down of velocity of circulation. This contraction of deposits and of their velocity, precipitated by distress selling, causes (3) *A fall in the level of prices*, in other words, a swelling of the dollar. Assuming, as above stated,

7

that this fall of prices is not interfered with by reflation or otherwise, there must be (4) *A still greater fall in the net worths of business*, precipitating bankruptcies and (5) *A like fall in profits*, which in a "capitalistic," that is, a private-profit society, leads the concerns which are running at a loss to make (6) *A reduction in output, in trade and in employment* of labor. These losses, bankruptcies and unemployment, lead to (7) *Hoarding and slowing down still more the velocity of circulation.*

The above eight changes cause (9) *Complicated disturbances in the rates of interest*, in particular, a fall in the nominal, or money, rates and a rise in the real, or commodity, rates of interest.

Evidently debt and deflation go far toward explaining a great mass of phenomena in a very simple logical way.

Hyman Minsky and James Tobin credited Fisher's Debt-Deflation Theory as a crucial precursor of their theories of macroeconomic financial instability.

Fisher explicitly ties loose money to over-indebtedness, fuelling speculation and asset bubbles:

Easy money is the great cause of over-borrowing. When an investor thinks he can make over 100 per cent per annum by borrowing at 6 per cent, he will be tempted to borrow, and to invest or speculate with the borrowed money. This was a prime cause leading to the over-indebtedness of 1929. Inventions and technological improvements created wonderful investment opportunities, and so caused big debts.

* * *

The public psychology of going into debt for gain passes through several more or less distinct phases: (a) the lure of big prospective dividends or gains in income in the remote future;

(b) the hope of selling at a profit, and realising a capital gain in the immediate future; (c) the vogue of reckless promotions, taking advantage of the habituation of the public to great expectations; (d) the development of downright fraud, imposing on a public which had grown credulous and gullible.

Fisher then sums up his theory of debt, deflation and instability in one paragraph:

> In summary, we find that: (1) economic changes include steady trends and unsteady occasional disturbances which act as starters for cyclical oscillations of innumerable kinds; (2) among the many occasional disturbances, are new opportunities to invest, especially because of new inventions; (3) these, with other causes, sometimes conspire to lead to a great volume of over-indebtedness; (4) this in turn, leads to attempts to liquidate; (5) these, in turn, lead (unless counteracted by reflation) to falling prices or a swelling dollar; (6) the dollar may swell faster than the number of dollars owed shrinks; (7) in that case, liquidation does not really liquidate but actually aggravates the debts, and the depression grows worse instead of better, as indicated by all nine factors; (8) the ways out are either laissez faire (bankruptcy) or scientific medication (reflation), and reflation might just as well have been applied in the first place.

The lender of last resort function of central banks and government support of the financial system through GSEs and fiscal measures are the modern mechanisms of reflation. Like Keynes, I suspect that Fisher saw reflation as a limited and temporary intervention rather than a long term sustained policy of credit expansion a la Greenspan/Bernanke.

I'm seriously worried that reflationary practice by Washington and the Fed in response to every market hiccup in recent decades was storing up a bigger debt deflation problem for the future. This very scary chart gives a measure of the threat in comparing Depression era total debt to GDP to today's much higher debt to GDP.

Certainly Washington and the Fed have been very enthusiastic and innovative in "reflating" the debt-sensitive financial, real estate, automotive and consumer sectors for the past many years. I'm tempted to coin a new noun for reflation enthusiasm: reflation?

Had Fisher observed the Greenspan/Bernanke Fed in action, he might have updated his theory with a revision. At some point, capital betrayed into unproductive works has to either be repaid or written off. If either is inhibited by reflation or regulatory forbearance, then a cost is imposed on productive works, whether through inflation, higher interest, diversion of consumption, or taxation to socialise losses. Over time that cost ultimately hollows out the real productive economy, leaving only bubble assets standing. Without a productive foundation, as reflation and forbearance reach their limits, those bubble assets must deflate.

Fisher's debt deflation theory was little recognised in his lifetime, probably because he was right in drawing attention to the systemic failures that precipitated the crash. Speaking truth to power isn't a ticket to popularity today either.

Thank you, Professor Roubini, for being brave enough to challenge orthodoxy before the crash, and for being generous enough to share your forum so that we can collectively address the causes and consequences of financial excess today.

Hat Tip: Robert Dimand, Department of Economics Brock University, St. Catharines, Ontario, Canada, for all of his efforts to rehabilitate Fisher's debt deflation theory.

Hat Tip: The Federal Reserve Bank of St Louis for making Fisher's entire 1933 paper from Econometrica available online in PDF.

Hat Tip: Guest on 2008-07-29 21:10:21 for the debt/GDP chart.

Hat Tip: SWK/Kilgores for suggesting a post on Fisher.

Hat Tip: Steve Phillips for tracing the Mills quote back and demonstrating it wasn't JS Mill as I originally attributed it.

Irving Fisher's Biography

Irving Fisher was born in Sugerties, New York on February 27, 1867, and – as his father who died of tuberculosis at age 53 – attended Yale University.

After receiving his degree, Fisher remained in Yale, where he taught mathematics as an assistant professor. In 1893, he married Margaret Hazard, a daughter from a wealthy family, and spent several months in Europe. After his return in 1895, he transferred from the mathematics department to the department of political economy, and in 1898, became a full professor of political economy at Yale within seven years of graduation. He stayed there during his entire career. Fisher was co-founder of both the Econometric Society and the American Economic Association.

Irving Fisher survived tuberculosis in his early 30s and developed a great interest in health and hygiene, writing a national best-seller titled "How to Live: Rules for Healthful Living Based on Modern Science." Fisher developed a system of index numbers that are used to this day by the FTSE to measure share value and the RPI. He sold the index to Sperry Rand and became a wealthy man, but lost a about $10 million in the stock market crash of 1929, having ruined his reputation by famously predicting a few days before the Crash: "Stock prices have reached what looks like a permanently high plateau." For months after the Crash, he continued to assure investors that a recovery was just around the corner." Fisher was so discredited by his 1929 pronouncements, and by the failure of the firm he had started, that few people took notice of his "debt-deflation" analysis of the Depression, and instead eagerly turned to the ideas of John Maynard Keynes. Fisher's debt-deflation scenario, however, made something of a comeback in the latter part of the twentieth century.

Fisher retired from Yale in 1935, and continued to live on support from his sister and her family. In 1940, his wife died, and in 1947, he developed cancer, from which he died on April 29 of that year, in New Haven, Connecticut. Fisher died of cancer in New York on April 29, 1947.

Fisher won first prize in a mathematics contest as a freshman. He took his PhD in 1892 on a dissertation entitled *"Mathematical Investigations in the Theory of Value and Prices"* which became a landmark in the development of mathematical economics and won immediate praise from Francis Y. Edgeworth and Vilfredo Pareto, two renowned economists.

Some fifty-five years later, Ragnar Frisch, a Norwegian economist at the University of Oslo and founding member of the Econometric Society, and winner of the 1969 Nobel Prize in Economic Science together with the Dutch economist, Jan Tinbergen, would say about Fisher: "He has been anywhere from a decade to two generations ahead of his time... it will be hard to find any single work that has been more influential than Fisher's dissertation." John Maynard Keynes wrote of Fisher as "the great grandparent" of The General Theory, "who first influenced me strongly towards regarding money as a 'real' factor" (Keynes, 1971-89, 14, pp. 203 n.; Dimand, 1995; Kregel, 1988).

"Irving Fisher was one of America's greatest mathematical economists and one of the clearest economics writers of all time. He had the intellect to use mathematics in virtually all his theories and the good sense to introduce it only after he had clearly explained the central principles in words. And he explained very well. Fisher's Theory of Interest [drawing heavily on John Rae and Eugen von Böhm-Bawerk, adding clarity and rigor to one of the most complex concepts in economics] is written so clearly that graduate economics students, who still study it today, often find that they can read—and understand—half the book in one sitting. With other writings in technical economics, this is unheard of."[2]

---

[2] Hannah Rasmussen for economics.about.com at http://economics. about.com/od/ famouseconomists/a/ irving _fisher.htm visited 2009-11-09

Fisher's *"The Purchasing Power of Money"* (1911) completely recasts the theory of money into his classical quantity-theory-of-money equation $MV + M'V' = PQ$, which made the purchasing power of money, the general price level P) completely determined by the stock of money in circulation M, its velocity of circulation $\dot{V}$, the volume of bank deposits M', their velocity of circulation V', and the total volume of transactions Q.

Fisher was also the first economist to distinguish clearly between real and nominal interest rates:

$$r = \frac{(1+i)}{(1+inflation)} - 1$$

where r is the real interest rate, is the nominal interest rate, and inflation is a measure of the increase in the price level. When inflation is sufficiently low, the real interest rate can be approximated as the nominal interest rate minus the expected inflation rate. The resulting equation bears his name.

Fisher translated his theory into a policy prescription of "100 percent money" (all bank deposits should be backed by 100 percent reserves rather than fractional reserves, used then and now by virtually all banking systems) on the grounds that such a policy would control large business cycles. According to the debt-deflation theory, a sequence of effects of the debt bubble bursting occurs:

1. Debt liquidation and distress selling.
2. Contraction of the money supply as bank loans are paid off.
3. A fall in the level of asset prices.
4. A still greater fall in the net worth of businesses, precipitating bankruptcies.
5. A fall in profits.
6. A reduction in output, in trade and in employment.
7. Pessimism and loss of confidence.
8. Hoarding of money.

The variety and quantity of Fisher's writings are enormous. His son, Irving Norton Fisher, compiled a 4,300-page bibliography of his known writings, *A Bibliography of the Writings of Irving Fisher* (1961); he also wrote a creditable biography, *My Father, Irving Fisher* (1956), that covers the essentials of his father's career. A valuable introduction to Fisher's many activities is William Fellner and others, *Ten Economic Studies in the Tradition of Irving Fisher* (1967); also Robert Loring Allen (1993), *Irving Fisher: a biography,* Cambridge, Massachusetts.: Blackwell Publishers.

Irving Fisher's primary publications:[3]

o   1892. *Mathematical Investigations in the Theory of Value and Prices.*
o   1896. *Appreciation and interest.*
o   1906. *The Nature of Capital and Income.*
o   1907. *The Rate of Interest.*
o   1910. *Introduction to Economic Science.*
o   1911. *The Purchasing Power of Money: Its Determination and Relation to Credit, Interest, and Crises.*
o   1911. *Elementary Principles of Economics.*
o   1915. *How to Live* (with Eugene Lyon Fisk).
o   1921, *The best form of index number, American Statistical Association Quarterly.*
o   1922. *The Making of Index Numbers.*
o   1923, "The Business Cycle Largely a `Dance of the Dollar'," *Journal of the American Statistical Society.*
o   1926, "A statistical relation between unemployment and price changes," *International Labour Review.* 1927, "A statistical method for measuring 'marginal utility' and testing the justice of a progressive income tax" in *Economic Essays Contributed in Honor of John Bates Clark.*
o   1930. *The Stock Market Crash and After.*
o   1930. *The Theory of Interest.*
o   1932. *Booms and Depressions* 1933, "The debt-deflation theory of great depressions," *Econometrica.*
o   1933. *Stamp Scrip.*
o   1935. *100% Money.*

---

[3] Ref.: *The Works of Irving Fisher.* edited by William J. Barber et al. 14 volumes London : Pickering & Chatto, 1996.

The Debt-Inflation Theory of Great Depressions

IRVING FISHER

Professor of Economics,
Yale University

October 1933

In *Booms and Depressions*,[4] I have developed, theoretically and statistically, what may be called a debt-deflation theory of great depressions. In the preface, I stated that the results "seem largely new," I spoke thus cautiously because of my unfamiliarity with the vast literature on the subject. Since the book was published its special conclusions have been widely accepted and, so far as I know, no one has yet found them anticipated by previous writers, though several, including myself, have zealously sought to find such anticipations. Two of the best-read authorities in this field assure me that those conclusions are, in the words of one of them, "both new and important."

Partly to specify what some of these special conclusions are which are believed to be new and partly to fit them into the conclusions of other students in this field, I am offering this paper as embodying, in brief, my present "creed" on the whole subject of so-called "cycle theory." My "creed" consists of 49 "articles" some of which are old and some new. I say "creed" because, for brevity, it is purposely expressed dogmatically and without proof. But it is not a creed in the sense that faith in it does not rest on

---

[4] Fisher, Irving. 1932. "Booms and Depressions: some first principles." New York: Adelphi Company.

evidence and that I am not ready to modify it on presentation of new evidence. On the contrary, it is quite tentative. It may serve as a challenge to others and as raw material to help them work out a better product.

Meanwhile the following is a list of my 49 tentative conclusions.

"Cycle-Theory" in General

1. The economic system contains innumerable variables – quantities of "goods" (physical wealth, property rights, and services), the prices of these goods, and their values (the quantities multiplied by the prices). Changes in any or all of this vast array of variables may be due to many causes. Only in imagination can all of these variables remain constant and be kept in equilibrium by the balanced forces of human desires, as manifested through "supply and demand."

2. Economic theory includes a study both of (a) such imaginary, ideal equilibrium – which may be stable or unstable – and (b) disequilibrium. The former is economic statistics; the latter, economic dynamics. So-called cycle theory is merely one part of the study of economic dis-equilibrium.

3. The study of dis-equilibrium may proceed in either of two ways. We may take as our unit for study an actual historical case of great dis-equilibrium, such as, say, the panic of 1873; or we may take as our unit for study any constituent tendency, such as, say, deflation, and discover its general laws, relations to, and combinations with, other tendencies. The former study resolves around events, or *facts*; the latter, around *tendencies*. The former is primarily economic history; the latter is primarily economic science. Both sorts of studies are proper and important. Each helps the other. The panic of 1873 can only be understood in the light of various tendencies involved – deflation and other; and deflation can only be understood in the light of the various historical manifestations – 1873 and other.

4. The old and apparently still persistent notion of "the " business cycle, as a single, simple, self-generating cycle (analogous to that of a pendulum swinging under influence of the single force of gravity) and as actually realized historically in regularly recurring crises, is a myth. Instead of one force there are many forces. Specifically, instead of one cycle, there are many co-existing cycles, constantly aggravating or neutralizing each other, as well as co-existing with many non-cyclical forces. In other words, while a cycle, conceived as a *fact*, or historical event, is non-existent, there are always innumerable cycles, long and short, big and little, conceived as *tendencies* (as well as numerous non-cyclical tendencies), any historical event being the resultant of all the tendencies then at work. Any one cycle, however perfect and like a sine curve it may tend to be, is sure to be interfered with by other tendencies.

5. The innumerable tendencies making mostly for economic dis-equilibrium may roughly be classified under three groups: (a) growth or trend tendencies, which are steady; (b) haphazard disturbances, which are unsteady; (c) cyclical tendencies, which are unsteady but steadily repeated.

6. There are two sorts of cyclical tendencies. One is "forced" or imposed on the economic mechanism from outside. Such is the yearly rhythm; also the daily rhythm. Both the yearly and the daily rhythm are imposed on us by astronomical forces from outside the economic organization; and there may be others such as from sun spots or transits of Venus. Other examples of "forced" cycles are the monthly and weekly rhythms imposed on us by custom and religion.

The second sort of cyclical tendency is the "free" cycle, not forced from outside, but self-generating, operating analogously to a pendulum or wave motion.

7. It is the "free" type of cycle which is apparently uppermost in the minds of most people when they talk of "the" business cycle. The yearly cycle, though it more nearly approaches a perfect cycle than any other, is seldom thought of as a cycle at all but referred to as "seasonal variation."

8. There may be equilibrium which, though stable, is so delicately poised that, after departure from it beyond certain limits, instability ensues, just as, at first, a stick may bend under strain, ready for all the time to bend back, until a certain point is reached, when it breaks. This simile [a comparison between two different things – Editor] probably applies when a debtor gets "broke," or when the breaking of many debtors constitutes a "crash," after which there is no coming back to the original equilibrium. To take another simile, such a disaster is somewhat like the capsizing" of a ship which, under ordinary conditions, is always near stable equilibrium but which, after being tipped beyond a certain angle, has no longer this tendency to return to equilibrium, but, instead, a tendency to depart further from it.

9. We may tentatively assume that, ordinarily and within wide limits, all, or almost all, economic variables tend, in a general way, toward a stable equilibrium. In our classroom expositions of supply and demand curves, we very properly assume that if the price, say, of sugar is above the point at which supply and demand are equal, it tends to fall; and if below, to rise.

10. Under such assumptions, and taking account of "economic friction," which is always present, it follows that, unless some outside force intervenes, any "free" oscillations about equilibrium must tend progressively to grow smaller and smaller, just as a rocking chair set in motion tends to stop. That is, while "forced" cycles, such as seasonal, tend to continue unabated in amplitude, ordinary "free" cycles tend to cease, giving way to equilibrium.

11. But the exact equilibrium thus sought is seldom reached and never long maintained. New disturbances are, humanly speaking, sure to occur, so that, in actual fact, any variable is almost always above or below the ideal equilibrium.

For example, coffee in Brazil may be over-produced, that is, may be more than it would have been if the producers had known in advance that it could not have been sold at a profit. Or there may be a shortage in the cotton crop. Or factory, or commercial inventories may be under or over the equilibrium point.

Theoretically there may be – in fact, at most times would be – over- or under-production, over- or under-consumption, over- or under-spending, over- or under-saving, over- or under-investment, and over or under everything else. It is absurd to assume that, for any long period of time, the variables in the economic organization, or any part of them, will "stay put," in perfect equilibrium, as to assume that the Atlantic Ocean can ever be without a wave.

12. The important variables which may, and ordinarily do, stand above or below equilibrium are: (a) capital items, such as homes, factories, ships, productive capacity generally, inventories, gold, money, credits, and debts; (b) income items, such as real income, volume of trade, shares traded; (c) price items, such as prices of securities, commodities, interest.

13. There may even be a *general* over-production and in either of two senses: (a) there may be, in general, at a particular point in time, over-large inventories or stocks on hand, or (b) there may be, in general, during a particular period of time, an over-rapid flow of production. The classical notion that over-production can only be relative as between different products is erroneous. Aside from the abundance or scarcity of particular products, relative to each other, production as a whole is relative to human desires and aversions, and can as a whole overshoot or undershoot the equilibrium mark.

In fact, except for brief moments, there must always be some degree of general over-production or general under-production and in both senses – stock and flow.

14. But, in practice, general over-production, as popularly imagined, has never, so far as I can discover, been a chief cause of great dis-equilibrium. The reason, or a reason, for the common notion of over-production is mistaking too little money for too much goods.

15. While any deviation from equilibrium of any economic variable theoretically may, and doubtless in practice does, set up some sort of oscillations, the important question is: Which of them have been sufficiently great disturbers to afford any substantial explanation of the great booms and depressions of history?

16. I am not sufficiently familiar with the long detailed history of these disturbances, nor with the colossal literature concerning their alleged explanations, to have reached any definitive conclusions as to the relative importance of all the influences at work. I am eager to learn from others.

17. According to my present opinion, which is purely tentative, there is some grain of truth in most of the alleged explanations commonly offered, but this grain is often small. Any of them may suffice to explain *small* disturbances, but all of them put together have probably been inadequate to explain big disturbances.

18. In particular, as explanations of the so-called business cycle, or cycles, when these are really serious, I doubt the adequacy of over-production, under-consumption, over-capacity, price-dislocation, mal-adjustment between agricultural and industrial prices, over-confidence, over-investment, over-saving, over-spending, and the discrepancy between saving and investment.

19. I venture the opinion, subject to correction on submission of further evidence, that, in the great booms and depressions, each of the above-named factors has played a subordinate rôle as compared with two dominant factors, namely *over-indebtedness* to start with and *deflation* following soon after; also that where any of the other factors do become conspicuous, they are often merely effects or symptoms of these two. In short, the big bad actors are debt disturbances and price-level disturbances.

While quite ready to change my opinion, I have, at present, a strong conviction that these two economic maladies, the debt disease and the price-level disease (or dollar disease), are, in the great booms and depressions, more important causes than all others put together.

20. Some of the other and usually minor factors often derive some importance when combined with one or both of the two dominant factors.

Thus over-investment and over-speculation are often important; but they would have far less serious results were they

21

not conducted with borrowed money. That is, over-indebtedness may lend importance to over-investment or to over-speculation.

The same is true as to over-confidence. I fancy that over-confidence seldom does any great harm except when, as, and if, it beguiles its victims into debt.

Another example is the mal-adjustment between agricultural and industrial prices, which can be shown to be a result of a change in the general price level.

21. Disturbances in these two factors – debt and the purchasing power of the monetary unit – will set up serious disturbances in all, or nearly all, other economic variables. On the other hand, if debt and deflation are absent, other disturbances are powerless to bring on crises comparable in severity to those of 1837, 1873, or 1929-33.

The Rôles of Debt and Deflation

22. No exhaustive list can be given of the secondary variables affected by the two primary ones, debt and deflation; but they include especially seven, making in all at least nine variables, as follows: debts, circulating media, their velocity of circulation, price levels, net worths, profits, trade, business confidences, interest rates.

23. *The chief interrelations between the nine chief factors may be derived deductively*, assuming, to start with, that general economic equilibrium is disturbed by only the one factor of over-indebtedness, and, in particular, assuming that there is no other influence, whether accidental or designed, tending to affect the price level.

24. Assuming, accordingly, that, at some point in time, a state of over-indebtedness exists, this will tend to lead to liquidation, through the alarm either of debtors or creditors or both. Then we may deduce the following chain of consequences in nine links: (1) *Debt liquidation* leads to *distress selling* and to (2) *Contraction of deposit currency*, as bank loans are paid off, and to a slowing down of velocity of circulation. This contraction of deposits and

of their velocity, precipitated by distress selling, causes (3) *A fall in the level of prices*, in other words, a swelling of the dollar. Assuming, as above stated, that this fall of prices is not interfered with by reflation or otherwise, there must be (4) *A still greater fall in the net worths of business*, precipitating bankruptcies and (5) *A like fall in profits,* which in a "capitalistic," that is, a private-profit society, leads the concerns which are running at a loss to make (6) *A reduction in output, in trade and in employment* of labor. These losses, bankruptcies, and unemployment, led to (7) *Pessimism and loss of confidence,* which in turn lead to (8) *Hording and slowing down still more the velocity of circulation.*

The above eight changes cause (9) *Complicated disturbances in the rates of interest,* in particular, as fall in the nominal, or money, rates and a rise in the real, or commodity, rates of interest.

Evidently debt and deflation go far toward explaining a great mass of phenomena in a very simply logical way.

25. The above chain causes, consisting of nine links, includes only a few of the interrelations between the nine factors. There are other demonstrable interrelations, both rational and empirical, and doubtless still others which cannot, yet, at least, be formulated at all.[5] There must also be many indirect relations involving variables not included among the nine groups.

26. One of the most important of such interrelations (and probably too little stressed in my *Booms and Depressions*) is the direct effect of lessened money, deposits, and their velocity, in curtailing trade, as evidenced by the fact that trade has been revived locally by emerging money without raising of the price level.

27. In actual chronology, the order of nine events is somewhat different from the above "logical" order, and there are reactions

---

[5] [Original footnote 1] Many of these interrelations have been shown statistically, and by many writers. Some, whch I have so shown and which fit in with the debt-deflation theory, are: that price-change, after a distributed lag, causes, or is followed by, corresponding fluctuations in the volume of trade, employment, bankruptcies, and rate of interest. The results as to price-change and unemployment are contained in Charts II and III, pp. 352-3. See references at the end of this article; also [original foot note 2 in the heading "Illustrated by the Depresson of 1929-33" below], regarding the charts.

and repeated effects. As stated in Appendix I of *Booms and Depressions:*

The following table of our nine factors, occurring and recurring (together with distress selling), gives a fairly typical, though still inadequate, picture of the cross-currents of a depression in the approximate order in which it is believed they usually occur. (The first occurrence of each factor and its sub-divisions is indicated in italics. The figures in parenthesis show the sequences in the original exposition.)

I.	(7)	Mild *Gloom* and Shock to *Confidence*
	(8)	Slightly *Reduced Velocity* of Circulation
	(1)	Debt *Liquidation*
II.	(9)	*Money Interest* on Safe Loans Falls
	(9)	But Money Interest on Unsafe Loans Rises
III.	(2)	*Distress Selling*
	(7)	More Gloom
	(3)	*Fall in Security Prices*
	(1)	More Liquidation
	(3)	*Fall in Commodity Prices*
IV.	(9)	*Real Interest Rises;* REAL DEBTS INCREASE
	(7)	More Pessimism and Distrust
	(1)	More Liquidation
	(2)	More Distress Selling
	(8)	More Reduction in Velocity
V.	(2)	More Distress Selling
	(2)	*Contraction of Deposit Currency*
	(3)	Further Dollar Enlargement
VI.	(4)	*Reduction in Net Worth*
	(4)	Increase in *Bankruptcies*
	(7)	More Pessimism and Distrust
	(8)	More Slowing in Velocity
	(1)	More Liquidation
VII.	(5)	*Decrease in Profits*
	(5)	*Increase in Losses*
	(7)	Increase in Pessimism

	(8)	Slower Velocity
	(1)	More Liquidation
	(6)	*Reduction in Volume of Stock Trading*
VIII.	(6)	*Decrease in Construction*
	(6)	*Reduction in Output*
	(6)	*Reduction in Trade*
	(6)	*Unemployment*
	(7)	More Pessimism
IX.	(8)	*Runs on Banks*
	(8)	*Banks Curtailing Loans* for Self-Protection
	(8)	*Banks Selling Investments*
	(8)	*Bank Failures*
	(7)	*Distrust Grows*
	(8)	More Hoarding
	(1)	More Liquidation
	(2)	More Distress Selling
	(3)	Further Dollar Enlargement

As has been stated, this order (or any order, for that matter) can be only approximate and subject to variations at different times and places. It represents my present guess as to how, if not too much interfered with, the nine factors selected for explicit study in this book are likely in most cases to fall in line.

But, as has also been stated, the idea of a single-line succession is itself inadequate, for while Factor (1) acts on (2), for instance, it also acts *directly* on (7), so that we really need a picture of subdividing streams or, better, an interacting network in which each factor may be pictured as influencing and being influenced by many or all of the others.

Paragraph 24 above gives a logical, and paragraph 27 a chronological, order of the chief variables put out of joint in a depression when once started by over-indebtedness.

28. But it should be noted that, except for the first and last in the "logical" list, namely debt and interest on debts, *all the fluctuations listed come about through a fall in prices.*

29. When over-indebtedness stands alone, that is, does *not* lead to a fall of prices, in other words, when its tendency to do so

is counter-acted by inflationary forces (whether by accident or design), the resulting "cycle" will be far milder and far more regular.

30. Likewise, when a deflation occurs from other than debt causes and without any great volume of debt, the resulting evils are much less. It is the combination of both – the debt disease coming first, then precipitating the dollar disease – which works the greatest havoc.

31. The two diseases act and react on each other. Pathologists are now discovering that a pair of diseases are sometimes worse than either or than the mere sum of both, so to speak. And we all know that a minor disease may lead to a major one. Just as a bad cold leads to pneumonia, so over-indebtedness leads to deflation.

32. And, vice versa, deflation caused by the debt reacts on the debt. Each dollar of debt still unpaid becomes a bigger dollar, and if the over-indebtedness with which we started was great enough, the liquidation of debts cannot keep up with the fall of prices which it causes. In that case, the liquidation defeats itself. While it diminishes the number of dollars owed, it may not do so as fast as it increases the value of each dollar owed. Then, *the very effort of individuals to lessen their burden of debts increases it, because of the mass effect of the stampede to liquidate in swelling each dollar owed.* Then we have the great paradox which, I submit, is the chief secret of most, if not all, great depressions: *The more the debtors pay, the more they owe.* The more the economic boat tips, the more it tends to tip. It is not tending to right itself, but is capsizing.

33. But if the over-indebtedness is not sufficiently great to make liquidation thus defeat itself, the situation is different and simpler. It is then more analogous to stable equilibrium; the more the boat rocks the more it will tend to right itself. In that case, we have a truer example of a cycle.

34. In the "capsizing" type in particular, the worst of it is that real incomes are so rapidly and progressively reduced. Idle men and idle machines spell lessened production and lessened real income, the central factor in all economic science. Incidentally

26

this under-production occurs at the very time that there is the illusion of over-production.

35. In this rapid survey, I have not discussed what constitutes over-indebtedness. Suffice it here to note that (a) over-indebtedness is always relative to other items, including national wealth and income and the gold supply, which last is specially important, as evidenced by the recent researches of Warren and Pearson; and (b) it is not a mere one-dimensional magnitude to be measured simply by the number of dollars owed. It must also take account of the distribution in time of the sums coming due. Debts due at once are more embarrassing than debts due years hence; and those payable at the option of the creditor, than those payable at the convenience of the debtor. Thus debt embarrassment is great for call loans and for early maturities.

For practical purposes, we may roughly measure the total national debt embarrassment by taking the total sum currently due, say within the current year, including rent, taxes, interest, installments, sinking fund requirements, maturities and any other definite or rigid commitments for payment on principal.

Illustrated by the Depression of 1929-33[6]

---

[6] Note to the charts in the Appendix:

Chart I shows: (1) the price level (P) and (2) its percentage rate of rise or fall (P'). When the last named is lagged with the lag distributed according to a probability curve so that the various P''s overlap and cumulate we get (line over) P', as in Charts II and III. This (line over) P' is virtually a lagged average of the P''s.

Charts II and *III* show: P' contrasted with employment (E). (Line over) P' may be considered as what employment would be if controlled *entirely* by price-change.

Chart IV shows the Swedish official (retail) weekly index number contrasted with the American weekly wholesale and monthly retail indexes.

Chart V shows the estimated internal debt in the United States contrasted with the estimated total money value of wealth. The unshaded extensions of the bars upward show what the 1933 figures would be if enlarged 75 per cent to translate them into 1929 dollars (according to the index numbers of wholesale commodity prices).

Chart VI shows estimated "fixed" annual charges (actually collected) contrasted with estimated national income. The unshaded extensions of the

27

36. The depression out of which were are now (I trust) emerging is an example of a debt-deflation depression of the most serious sort. The debts of 1929 were the greatest known, both nominally and really, up to that time.

They were great enough not only to "rock the boat" but to start it capsizing. By March, 1933, liquidation had reduced the debts about 20 per cent, but had increased the dollar about 75 per cent, so that the *real* debt, that is the debt as measured in terms of commodities, was increased by 40 per cent [(100% − 20%) x (100% + 75%) = 140%]. Note Chart V.

37. Unless some counteracting cause comes along to prevent the fall in the price level, such a depression as that of 1929-33 (namely when the more the debtors pay the more they owe) tends to continue, going deeper, in a vicious spiral, for many years. There is then no tendency of the boat to stop tipping until it has capsized. Ultimately, of course, but only after almost universal bankruptcy, the indebtedness must cease to grow greater and being to grow less. Then comes recovery and a tendency for a new boom-depression sequence. This is a so-called "natural" way out of a depression, via needless and cruel bankruptcy, unemployment, and starvation.

38. On the other hand, if the foregoing analysis is correct, it is always economically possible to stop or prevent such a depression simply by reflating the price level up to the average level at which outstanding debts were contracted by existing debtors and assumed by existing creditors, and then maintain that level unchanged.

That the price level is controllable is not only claimed by monetary theorists but has recently been evidenced by two great events: (1) Sweden has now for nearly two years maintained a stable price level, practically always within 2 per cent of the chosen par and usually within 1 per cent. Note Chart IV. (2) The fact that immediate reversal of deflation is easily achieved by the

---

bars upward show what the 1932 figures would be if enlarged 56 percent to translate them into 1929 dollars.

Charts VII and *VIII* show the chief available statistics before and after March 4, 1933, grouped in the order indicated in Article 27 above.

use, or even the prospect of use, of appropriate instrumentalities has just been demonstrated by President Roosevelt. Note Charts VII and VIII.

39. Those who imagine that Roosevelt's avowed reflation is not the cause of our recovery but that we had "reached the bottom anyway" are very much mistaken. At any rate, they have given no evidence, so far as I have seen, that we had reached the bottom. And if they are right, my analysis must be woefully wrong. According to all the evidence, under that analysis, debt and deflation, which had wrought havoc up to March 4, 1933, were then stronger than ever and, if let alone, would have wreaked greater wreckage than ever, after march 4. Had no "artificial respiration" been applied, we would soon have seen general bankruptcies of the mortgage guarantee companies, savings banks, life insurance companies, railways, municipalities, and states. By the time the Federal Government would probably have become unable to pay its bills without resort to the printing press, which would itself have been a very belated and unfortunate case of artificial respiration. If even then our rulers should still have insisted on "leaving recovery to nature" and should still have refused to inflate in any way, should vainly have tried to balance the budget and discharge more government employees, to raise taxes, to float, or try to float, more loans, they would soon have ceased to be our rulers. For we would have insolvency of our national government itself, and probably some form of political revolution without waiting for the next legal election. The mid-west farmers had already begun to defy the law.

40. If all this is true, it would be as silly and immoral to "let nature take her course" as for a physician to neglect a case of pneumonia. It would also be a libel on economic science, which has its therapeutics as truly as medical science.

41. If reflation can now so easily and quickly reverse the deadly down-swing of deflation after nearly four years, when it was gathering increased momentum, it would have been still easier, and at any time, to have stopped it earlier. In fact, under President Hoover, recovery was apparently well started by the Federal Reserve open-market purchases, which revived prices and

business from May to September 1932. The efforts were not kept up and recovery was stopped by various circumstances, including the political "campaign of fear."

It would have been still easier to have prevented the depression almost altogether. In fact, in my opinion, this would have been done had Governor Strong of the Federal Reserve Bank of New York lived, or had his policies been embraced by other banks and the Federal Reserve Board and pursued consistently after his death.[7] In that case, there would have been nothing worse than the first crash. We would have had the debt disease, but not the dollar disease – the bad cold but not the pneumonia.

42. If the debt-deflation theory of great depressions is essentially correct, the question of controlling the price level assumes a new importance; and those in the drivers' seats – the Federal Reserve Board and the Secretary of the Treasury, or, let us hope, a special stabilization commission – will in future be held to a new accountability.

43. Price level control, or dollar control, would not be a panacea. Even with an ideally stable dollar, we would still be exposed to the debt disease, to the technological-unemployment disease, to over-production, price-dislocation, over-confidence, and many other minor diseases. To find the proper therapy for these diseases will keep economists busy long after we have exterminated the dollar disease.

Debt Starters

44. The over-indebtedness hitherto presupposed must have had its starters. It may be started by many causes, of which the most common appears to be *new opportunities to invest at a big*

---

[7] [Original note 3] Eventually, however, in order to have avoided depression, the gold standard would have had to be abandoned or modified (by devaluation); for, with the gold standard as of 1929, the price levels at that time could not have been maintained indefinitely in the face of: (1) the "scramble for gold" due to the continued extension of the gold standard to include nation after nation; (2) the increasing volume of trade; and (3) the prospective insufficiency of the world gold supply.

prospective profit, as compared with ordinary profits and interest, such as through new innovations, new industries, development of new resources, opening of new lands or new markets. Easy money is the great cause of over-borrowing. When an investor thinks he can make over 100 per cent per annum by borrowing at 6 per cent, he will be tempted to borrow, and to invest or speculate with borrowed money. This was a prime cause leading to the over-indebtedness of 1929. Inventions and technological improvements created wonderful investment opportunities, and so cause big debts. Other causes were the left-over war debts, domestic and foreign, public and private, the reconstruction loans to foreigners, and the low interest policy adopted to help England get back on the gold standard in 1925.

Each case of over-indebtedness has its own starter or set of starters. The chief starters of the over-indebtedness leading up to the crisis of 1837 were connected with lucrative investment opportunities from developing the West and Southwest in real estate, cotton, canal building (led by the Erie Canal), steamboats, and turnpikes, opening up each side of the Appalachian Mountains to the other. For the over-indebtedness leading up to the crisis of 1873, the chief starters were the exploitation of railways and of western farms following the Homestead Act. The over-indebtedness leading up to the panic of 1893 was chiefly relative to the gold base which had become too small, because of the injection of too much silver. But the panic of 1893 seems to have had less of the debt ingredient than in most cases, though deflation played a leading rôle.

The starter may, of course, be wholly or in part the pendulum-like back-swing or reaction in recovery from a preceding depression as commonly assumed by cycle theorists. This, of itself, would tend to leave the next depression smaller than the last.

45. When the starter consists of new opportunities to make unusually profitable investments, the bubble of debt tends to be blown bigger and faster than when the starter is great misfortune causing merely non-productive debts. The only notable exception

is a great war and even then chiefly it leads *after it is over* to productive debts for reconstruction purposes.

46. This is quite different from the common naïve opinions of how war results in depression. If the present interpretation is correct, the World War need never have led to a great depression. It is very true that much or most of the inflations could not have been helped because of the exigencies of governmental finance, but the subsequent undue deflations could probably have been avoided entirely.

47. The public psychology of going into debt for gain passes through several more or less distinct phases: (a) the lure of big prospective dividends or gains in *income* in the remote future; (b) the hope of selling at a profit, and realizing a *capital* gain in the immediate future; (c) the vogue of reckless promotions, taking advantage of the habituation of the public to great expectations; (d) the development of downright fraud, imposing on a public which had grown credulous and gullible.

When it is too late the dupes discover scandals like the Hatry, Krueger, and Insull scandals. At least one book has been written to prove that crises are due to frauds of clever promoters. But probably these frauds could never have become so great without the original starters of real opportunities to invest lucratively. There is probably always a very real basis for the "new era" psychology before it runs away with its victims. This was certainly the case before 1929.

48. In summary, we find that: (1) economic changes include steady trends and unsteady occasional disturbances which act as starters for cyclical oscillations of innumerable kinds; (2) among the many occasional disturbances, are new opportunities to invest, especially because of new inventions; (3) these, with other causes, sometimes conspire to lead to a great volume of over-indebtedness; (4) this, in turn, leads to attempts to liquidate; (5) these, in turn, lead (*unless counter-acted by reflation*) to falling prices or a swelling dollar; (6) the dollar may swell faster than the number of dollars owed shrinks; (7) in that case, liquidation does not really liquidate but actually aggravates the debts, and the depression grows worse instead of better, as indicated by all nine

factors; (8) the ways out are either *via laissez faire* (bankruptcy), or scientific medication (reflation), and reflation might just as well have been applied in the first place.

49. The general correctness of the above "debt-deflation theory of great depressions" is, I believe, evidenced by experience in the present and previous great depressions. Future studies by others will doubtless check up on this opinion. One way is to compare different countries simultaneously. If the "debt-deflation theory" is correct, the infectiousness of depressions internationally is chiefly due to a common gold (or other) monetary standard and there should be found little tendency for a depression to pass from a deflating to an inflating, a stabilizing, country.

Some New Features

As stated at the outset, several features of the above analysis are, as far as I know, new. Some of these are too unimportant or self-evident to stress. The one (No. 32 above; also 36) which I do venture to stress most is the theory that when over-indebtedness is so great as to depress prices faster than liquidation, the mass effort to get out of debt sinks us more deeply into debt.[8] I would

---

[8] [Original footnote 4] This interaction between liquidation and deflation did not occur to me until 1931, although, with others, I had since 1909 been stressing the fact that deflation tended toward depressoin and inflation toward boom.

This debt-deflation theory was first stated in my lecture at Yale in 1931, and first stated publicly before the American Association for the Advancement of Science, on January 1, 1932. It is fully set forth in my *Booms and Depressions*, 1932, and some special features of my general view on cycle theory in "Business Cycles as Facts or Tendencies" in *Economische Opstellen Aangeboden aan Prof. C.A. Verrijn Stuart*, Haarlem, 1931. Certain sorts of disequilibrium are discussed in other writings. The rôle of the lag between real and nominal interest is discussed in *The Purchasing Power of Money*, Macmillan, New York, 1911; and more fully in *The Theory of Interest*, Macmillan, New York, 1930, as well as the effects of iequality of foresight. Some statistical verification will be found in "Our Unstable Dollar and the So-called Business Cycle," *Journal of the American Statistical Association*, June

also like to emphasize the whole logical articulation of the nine factors, of which debt and deflation are the two chief (Nos. 23, 24, and 28, above). I would call attention to *new investment opportunities* as the important "starter" of over-indebtedness (Nos. 44, 45). Finally, I would emphasize the important corollary, of the debt-deflation theory, that great depressions are curable and preventable through reflation and stabilization (Nos. 38-42).

Yale University

EDITOR'S NOTE

Irving Fisher published his "The Debt-Deflation Theory of Great Depressions" as an analysis of past events in 1933, still hopeful of a turnaround. When this did not occur, he presented a monetary system's solution in his book two years later: "100% Money" (1935). Fisher's own brief summary entitled"**100% Money and the Public Debt**" (1936) is also available from this publisher.

1925, pp. 179-202, and "The Relation of Employment to the Price Level" (address given before a section of the American Association for the Advancement of Science, Atlantic City, N.J., December 28, 1932, and later published in *Stabilization of Employment*, edited by Charles F. Roos, The Principia Press, Inc., Bloomingdale, Ind., 1933, pp. 152-159). See Charts I, II, III. Some statistical verification will be found in the *Stock Market Crash and After*, Macmillan, New York, 1930.

A selected bibliography of the writings of others is given in Appendix III of *Booms and Depressions*, Adelphi Company, New York, 1932. This bibliography omitted Veblen's *Theory of Business Enterprises*, Charles Scribner's Sons, New York, 1904, Chapter VII in which, Professor Wesley C. Mitchell points out, probably comes nearest to the debt-deflation theory. Hawtrey's writings eem the next nearest. Professor Alvin H. Hansen informs me that Professor Paxson, of the American History Department of the Univeristy of Wisconsin, in a course on the History of the West some twenty years ago, stressed the debt factor and its relation to deflation. But so gar as I know, no one hitherto has pointed out how debt liquidation defeats itself via deflation nor several other features of the present "creed". If any clear-cut anticipation exists, it can never have been prominently set forth, for even the word "debt" is missing in the indexes of the treatises on the subject.

Charts

The following eight charts are all on the "ratio scale" excepting Charts II, III, V, VI, and curve P' of Chart I. The particular ratio scale used is indicated in each case.

It will be noted that in Charts VII and VIII all curves have a common ratio scale, as indicated by the inset at the right in both charts, except "Brokers' Loans" in Chart VII and "Failures Numbers," "Failures Liabilities," and "Shares Traded" in Chart VIII, which four curves have another, "reduced" i.e., smaller, common scale, as indicated by the inset at the left of Chart VIII.

It will be further noted that "Money in Circulation," "Failures Numbers," and "Failures Liabilities" are inverted.

The full details of (line over) P' in Charts II and III is derived from P' in Chart I and also how P' in Chart I is derived from P are given in "Our Unstable Dollar and the So-Called Business Cycle," *Journal of the American Statistical Association*, June, 1925.

Charts I and II

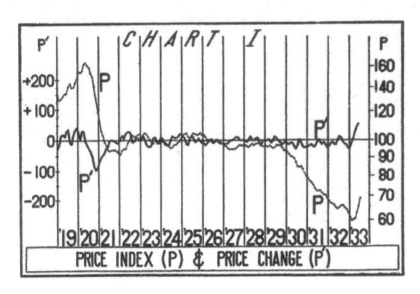

PRICE INDEX (P) & PRICE CHANGE (P')

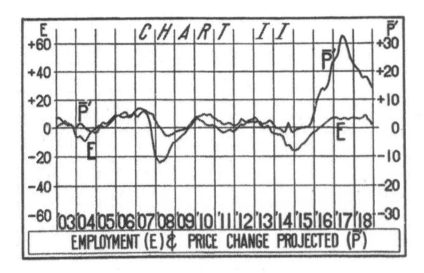

EMPLOYMENT (E) & PRICE CHANGE PROJECTED (P̄')

Charts III and IV

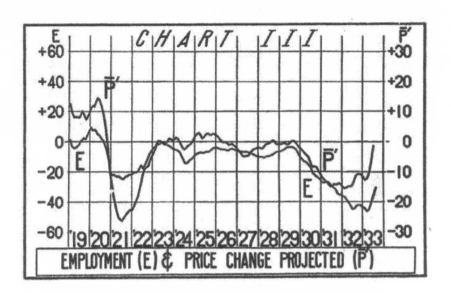

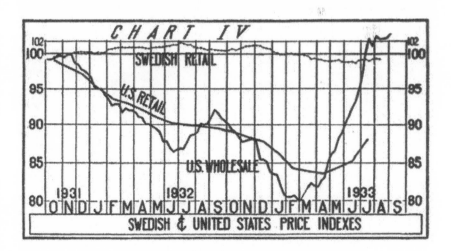

Chart V

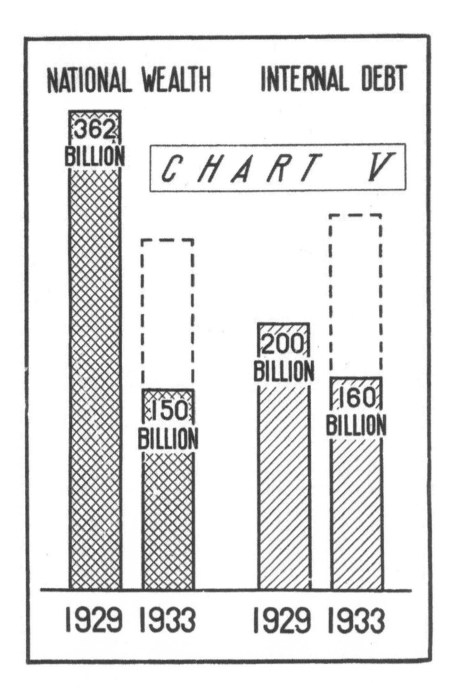

NATIONAL WEALTH   INTERNAL DEBT

362 BILLION

CHART V

150 BILLION

200 BILLION

160 BILLION

1929 1933   1929 1933

Chart VI

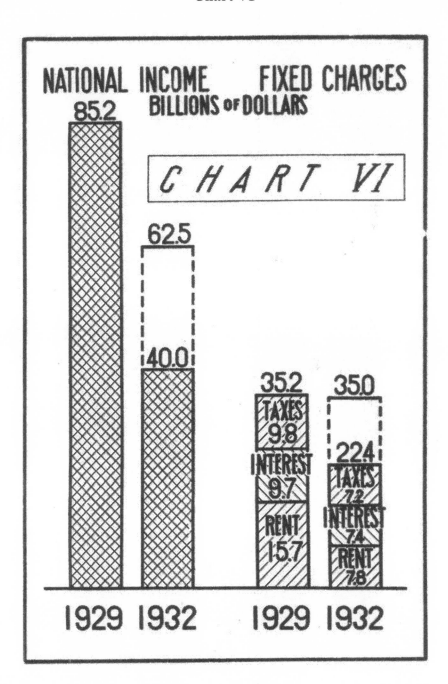

NATIONAL INCOME   FIXED CHARGES
BILLIONS of DOLLARS

CHART VI

85.2

62.5

40.0

35.2
TAXES 9.8
INTEREST 9.7
RENT 15.7

35.0
TAXES 7.2
INTEREST 7.4
RENT 7.8

1929 1932   1929 1932

Chart VII

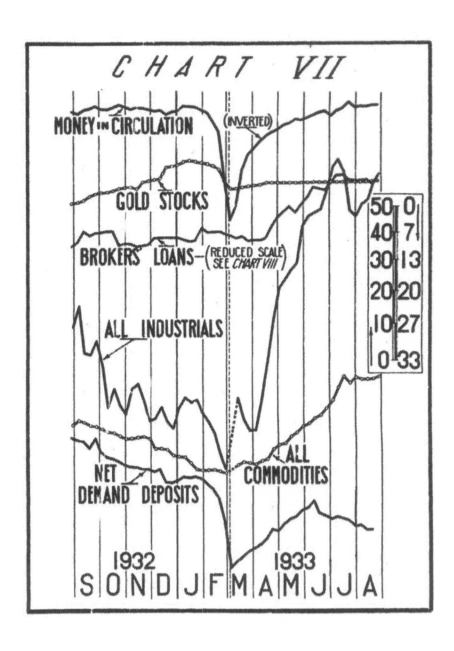

Chart VII

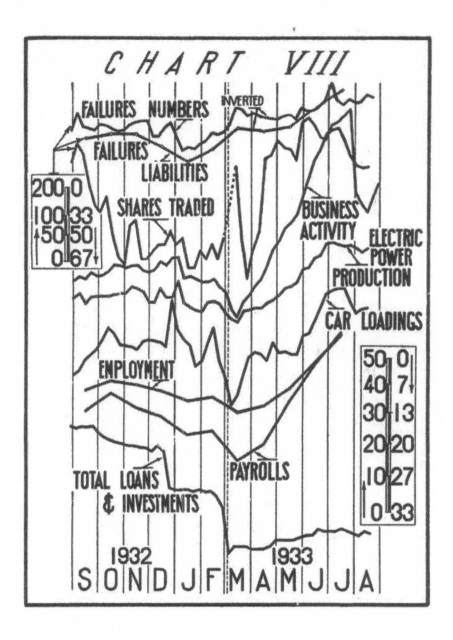

41

Made in the USA
Monee, IL
30 July 2021

74622176R00025